MW EDUCATIONAL

AF504063

THE A PLUS SERIES OF 11+ PRACTICE PAPERS

ENGLISH

Volume 2 Multiple Choice Format

INSTRUCTIONS FOR THE PERSON TAKING THE TESTS

Please read these instructions before you start the English tests

1. Do not begin any of the tests until you are instructed to do so. You will be allowed 45 minutes to do each test.

2. Try and answer as many questions as you can. If you find that you cannot answer a question, do not waste time trying to answer it. Leave that question and come back to it at the end if you have any time left.

3. This is a multiple-choice test. You should mark your answers on the answer sheet provided at the end of this booklet and not on the test paper.

4. To answer a question, draw a line <u>in pencil</u> across the box that is <u>next</u> to the correct answer. If you wish to change an answer, simply rub out your line and draw a fresh line in another box. Some examples have been done to help you.

5. Work as quickly as you can, taking care that you do not miss any questions out.

6. If you complete a test before the end of the allotted time, go back over your test, checking that you have not missed out any questions and check your answers

7. Once the test has begun, you are not allowed to ask any questions.

PAPER 1

Read the passage below and then answer the questions on it, by choosing the correct letter – a, b, c or d. Mark your answers on the separate answer sheet. It is a letter written by a soldier on the Western Front fighting in France during the 1st World War to his wife back in England.

Company C
3rd Armoured Division
France
12th July 1916

My Darling Rose,

It is now two months since I last saw you back in dear old England. I remember how green it all was - the fields and the trees. Here everything is a dark brown. It is the mud of the battlefield, which we can see wherever we look. The trees - what's left of them - don't have leaves and hardly any branches. It is a desolate sight with not a building left standing for miles around.

5 No doubt you will have heard our news from the newspapers about the disastrous battle that has just taken place here. I am fine, thank God, but many of my friends and comrades were not so fortunate. We were ordered to advance at dawn towards the enemy lines. Dutifully we left our trenches - glad to get away from the stench and squalor – but no sooner had we advanced into no man's land than we came under intense fire from the enemy. Many men were shot down like
10 rabbits by the enemy's machine guns. Thousands and thousands in fact. A great tragedy.
My own dear friend Tommy Harris fell almost next to me. Sadly he died. In the end we had to lie flat in the mud to save our lives. Then it was several hours before we were able to retreat back to the safety of our trenches. I have tried to clean myself as best as I can with the little water I had. I shall never forget this day.
15 I hope and pray that I will survive this horror and will soon be back in England again with you.

With love from your darling Walter

1)   What do you think "dear" means when he is writing about England?
    (a)   It is dear as in expensive   (b)   It is dear to his heart
    (c)   It is the dear as in writing a letter   (d)   None of these things

2)   Why do you think everything is "dark brown" (line 2)?
    (a)   The houses are painted that colour   (b)   Battlefields are always that colour
    (c)   The uniforms are that colour   (d)   The grass has been destroyed

3)   What does "desolate" (line 4) mean?
    (a)   horrible   (b)   beautiful   (c)   ugly   (d)   barren

4)   Why were no buildings left standing "for miles around" (line 4)?
    (a)   There was an earthquake   (b)   They fell down
    (c)   They were blown up   (d)   They knocked them down

5)   What does "dawn" (line 7) mean?
    (a) Day break   (b) Sunset   (c) Day time   (d) Twilight

6)   What were the men going to attack?
    (a) A building   (b) The enemy lines   (c) A gun placement   (d) A tank

7) Another word for "squalor" (line 8) would be:-
(a) Mud (b) Smell (c) Dirt (d) Mess

8) How did Walter manage to stay alive?
(a) By lying in the mud (b) By retreating (c) By crawling (d) By going forward

9) The writer of the letter seems to be which of the following?
(a) Worried (b) Upset (c) Unhappy (d) Happy

10) In what month was he last back in England?
(a) April (b) May (c) June (d) July

A pronoun is a word that is used instead of a noun. *E.g. He, she or it.* **Find the pronoun in each of these sentences and mark your answers on the separate answer sheet.**

11) I didn't like the way the man spoke to David.

12) When the children saw the monster, they quickly ran away.

13) After finishing supper, we hurried to watch the TV.

14) The rules state that you are not allowed to run on the pavement.

15) Our friends behaved very well at the party.

16) The athlete was cross with himself for tripping up in the race.

17) "What a rude girl!" announced the lady. "She wouldn't move out of the way".

18) "Who saw the intruder?" asked the police officer.

In the sentences below there are two words in brackets which sound the same, but which are spelt differently. Find the word that you think is the correct one for each sentence and mark your answers on the separate answer sheet.

19) (They're, their) going on holiday tomorrow.

20) I (herd, heard) the howling of the wolves at the zoo.

21) Sometimes my brother (growns, groans) if he has homework to do.

22) The child kept asking his parent (whether, weather) it was time yet.

23) In olden times pirates would bury their (hoard, horde) of treasure.

24) My sister heard that she has (past, passed) her exams.

25) The (pair, pear) of thieves ran when they heard the police siren.

26) On the waste land near my home, they have started a building (sight, site).

27) The teenager was (thrown, throne) out of the cinema for being under-age.

28) Yesterday, after supper, my grandfather told us some ghostly (tails, tales).

TURN OVER

Below is an extract taken from a magazine showing which programmes are on different TV channels on the evening of 1st July. After looking at the programme listings and times, answer the questions below. Mark your answers on the separate answer sheet.

<u>TV GUIDE WEDNESDAY EVENING - 1ST JULY</u>

	<u>6 - 7 PM</u>	<u>7 - 8 PM</u>	<u>8 -9 PM</u>	<u>9 -10 PM</u>
CHANNEL 1	Beverly Hills 90210	Spellbound	Space: Above & Beyond	The Outer Limits
CHANNEL 2	You Rang M'Lord	Morecambe & Wise	Film: Carry on Loving	
SCIENCE-FICTION		Battlestar Galactica	Film: House of the Long Shadows	
LIFESTYLE	Bewitched	Brookside	Street Legal	Film: Nurses on the Line
ENCORE	Charlie Chan	Department S	Sapphire & Steele	Randall and Hopkirk (deceased)
FUN CHANNEL	Batman	A Word In Your Ear	Only When I Laugh	Father Dowling Mysteries
EXPLORATION	Beyond 2000	Wild Things	Mysterious Universe	Unexplained

29) How many different programmes are listed above?
(a) five   (b) seven   (c) twenty-two   (d) twenty-five

30) The abbreviation for Science Fiction is: -
(a) SF   (b) Sci-Fi   (c) Si-Fi   (d) Sc-Fi

31) What programme is on the Lifestyle channel between 7 and 8 pm?
(a) Brookside   (b) Spellbound   (c) Department S   (d) Wild Things

32) On which channel would you be watching the film "House of the Long Shadows"?
(a) Channel 1   (b) Lifestyle   (c) Science Fiction   (d) Exploration

33) What <u>channel</u> has a programme that has the name of a priest in its title?
(a) UK Channel   (b) Encore   (c) Exploration   (d) Fun Channel

34) Name the programme that has a jewel and a type of metal in its title.
(a) Charlie Chan   (b) Morecambe & Wise
(c) Sapphire & Steele   (d) Randall & Hopkirk

35) What year is mentioned in one of the programmes?
(a) 5   (b) 10   (c) 2000   (d) 90210

36) The word "deceased" from the Encore channel programme called "Randall and Hopkirk (deceased)" means: -
(a) Lost   (b) Confused   (c) Dead   (d) Partners

37)   What is the letter 'M' an abbreviation for in the Channel 2 programme "You Rang M' Lord"?
(a) Me   (b) My   (c) Mine   (d) Mister

38)   What is the name of the programme that has a part of the body in its title?
(a) Spellbound   (b) Batman   (c) Wild Things   (d) A Word In Your Ear

39)   Which programme has the name of an English seaside resort in its title?
(a) Charlie Chan   (b) Morecambe & Wise
(b) Battlestar Galactica   (d) Beverley Hills 910210

In the lines below the words in the sentences are jumbled up. Rearrange these sentences so that they read sensibly, then decide which word would <u>come last</u> in the rearranged sentence. Mark your answers on the separate answer sheet. The first word of the sentence has been underlined for you. You can write out the correct order of words first in the space underneath each sentence if you wish. *An example has been done for you.*

E.g.   *bakers to <u>I</u> went the buy some to bread*

Answer: *I went to the bakers to buy some <u>bread</u>.*

40)   come and told me watch the <u>My</u> father to game

41)   toast with egg I had and bacon <u>For</u> breakfast

42)   the park in Summer the <u>We</u> go to

43)   the way was spoken <u>I</u> like to I didn't

44)   friend my birthday <u>My</u> remembered best

45)   they played listening which the music <u>We</u> to enjoyed

46)   kind was frightened girl <u>The</u> rescued by the animal

47)   strawberry picking I and go brother <u>Every</u> my year

END OF TEST PAPER ONE

<u>PAPER 2</u>

Read through the passage below and then answer the questions that follow it. Mark your answers on the separate answer sheet. It is about the Indian leader, Mahatma Gandhi.

Mahatma Gandhi was born of Hindu parents in the state of Gujarat in India in 1869. After completing his schooling he was sent to London to study law. In 1891 he was "called to the bar" and became a barrister. He then emigrated to South Africa where he actively became involved in protecting the rights of fellow Indians living there. It was in this country that he
5   began to develop a belief in the idea of fighting against injustice by the act of "Passive Resistance". This meant not obeying certain laws if they were cruel and inhuman such as the policy of segregating people according to the colour of their skin. As a result of this belief he was put into prison on many occasions.

      After several years he returned to India in 1914, where he led the struggle for Indians to
10 gain independence from British rule. He was firmly in favour of protesting through non-violent means and by showing tolerance to peoples of other beliefs. If there was violence committed by Hindus or Muslims against the British he would fast until the violence had ceased. In 1930 he led the famous "Salt March" across India to protest against the law forbidding Indians to produce their own salt.

15   In 1947 India gained independence from British rule, but the violence continued when India was split into two distinct countries - India, which contained mainly Hindu believers, and Pakistan, which contained mainly Muslim believers. Once again he fasted to try and end the violence between the two factions. Then sadly in January 1948 he was assassinated in Delhi as he was on his way to evening prayers. His death was not in vain however as many
20 people the world over have followed his lead and have tried to bring about change in their countries through non-violence. One of his most famous sayings is: "Non-violence is the greatest force at the disposal of mankind. It is mightier than the mightiest weapon of destruction devised by the ingenuity of man".

1)   Where was Gandhi born?
     (a) London   (b) South Africa   (c) India   (d) Pakistan

2)   "Emigrated" (line 3) means: -
     (a)   Travelling to another country   (b)   Sending things to another country
     (c)   Going to live in another country   (d)   Studying in another country

3)   What is "segregating people according to the colour of their skin" (line 7) sometimes called?
     (a)   Racial mixing   (b)   Racial attraction
     (c)   Racial discretion   (d)   Racial discrimination

4)   What part of speech is "independence" (line 10)?
     (a) Verb   (b) Adverb   (c) Adjective   (d) Noun

5)   If you "fast" (line 12) you: -
     (a)   Stop speaking for a while   (b)   Stop eating for a while
     (c)   Stop travelling for a while   (d)   None of these

6)   How many years after Gandhi returned to India from South Africa did India gain Independence from British rule?
     (a) 33 years   (b) 35 years   (c) 38 years   (d) 39 years

7)   What does "assassinated" (line 18) mean?
      (a)   Shooting someone   (b)   Being killed through violence
      (c)   Dying through shock   (d)   Dying naturally

8)   "His death was not in vain" (line 19) means: -
      (a)   It wasn't meant to happen   (b)   It wasn't at the right time
      (c)   It wasn't in the right place   (d)   It wasn't a waste

9)   What does "disposal" (line 22) mean in this context?
      (a) Opportunity   (b) Use   (c) Freedom   (d) Waste

In the sentences below, one of the following types of punctuation has been missed out: - comma (,) full stop (.) apostrophe (') question mark (?) inverted commas (""). Work out which type of punctuation mark is missing and mark your answers on the separate answer sheet.

10)   "I cant come to your party," said Stuart.

11)   "Where is your pullover " asked Mum.

12)   The man ate some cheese bread and pickle for his lunch.

13)   They all enjoyed their visit to the pantomime

14)   Why haven't you done your homework? enquired Dad.

15)   The children liked the film, Raiders Of The Lost Ark.

16)   "Dont speak to me like that!" shouted the teacher.

17)   Each child wore a coat, a hat a scarf and some boots.

18)   Her father said, "What time shall I pick you up"

19)   Lately, the weather has started to get much colder

Adverbs are words that describe verbs. In the sentences below find the adverb and mark your choices on the separate answer sheet. *An example has been done for you.*

E.g.   *The large man was running <u>slowly</u> as he was exhausted.*

20)   We couldn't find the treasure despite looking hard for it.

21)   "Don't walk so slowly!" shouted the teacher to the child.

22)   The girl was hardly clever enough to solve the puzzle.

23)   My best friend failed the test badly.

24)   The soldiers fought bravely against the enemy.

25)   Our neighbour worked lovingly on his garden.

26)   I couldn't understand the way they laughed mockingly at him.

27)   The bus arrived later than expected

28)   It was quite nice playing in the snow last year.

29)   They once visited the Thames Barrier.

TURN OVER

Robert walked carefully up the brightly carpeted staircase towards the dining room, taking care not to spill any of the boiling–hot soup that he was carrying.
"Take care, Master Robert!" ordered the senior butler, Mr. Walker. "His Lordship will not tolerate sloppiness from any of his servants".
5   Robert, who had only just celebrated his tenth birthday, carefully placed the tray on the side table, next to the gleaming silverware, glancing wide-eyed at all the luxury before him.
"Will that be all Mr. Walker?" enquired Robert", who by now was quite out of breath.
"Yes. Robert" replied the flustered butler. "You may retire downstairs and stay in your room until I personally call for you".
10 Mr. Walker seemed more agitated than usual, but it was obvious that he was in a flap because the guest of honour at tonight's dinner party, would be none other than His Majesty, King Edward VII! Robert, like the rest of the staff in Lord Milton's household was very excited by the prospect of seeing the King in the flesh. He had only been working as a junior servant in the household for less than six months, but now he was finally settled and happy in his life.
15 Previously, Robert had lived in a squalid, unlit and derelict warehouse next to the river with several other orphaned urchins. But ever since that fateful day when he had saved the life of Lord Milton's daughter, Emily, by rescuing her from drowning, his life had improved for the better.
As Robert entered the servant's quarters he could see a group gathered around the fire in the kitchen.
"I bet he leaves the fish", argued Sam Willis, one of the servants.
20 "A penny he doesn't!" replied Sally Morton, the chamber maid.
"That's enough!" interrupted Mrs. Dawson, the head cook. "I want you all in place as soon as that bell there rings!"
Almost immediately, the bell rang and there was a flurry of activity. Robert moved out of the way quickly and waited for his call.

30) How many people are mentioned in this extract?
(a) Seven   (b) Eight   (c) Nine   (d) Ten

31) Who do you think "His Lordship" was (line 3)?
(a) The King   (b) The butler   (c) The owner of the house   (d) Sam Willis

32) Which of these words best describes Robert's state after carrying the soup up the stairs?
(a) Worried   (b) Breathless   (c) Tired   (d) Elation

33) Why was Mr. Walker so agitated on that particular day?
(a) Robert spilt the soup   (b) He was out of breath
(c) He was being sloppy   (d) The King was coming to dinner

34) Where in the house do you think Robert's room was situated?
(a) Downstairs   (b) Next to the dining room   (c) In a warehouse   (d) Upstairs

35) How long had Robert been working in the household?
(a) One month   (b) Two months   (c) Five months   (d) Seven months

36) What part of speech is the word "squalid" (line 15)?
(a) Noun   (b) Adjective   (c) Verb   (d) Adverb

37)   A person who is an "orphan" (line 16) means: -
(a) Someone who is very poor   (b) Someone who has nowhere to live
(c) Someone who has no parents   (d) Someone who steals from other people

38)   If you are an "urchin" (line 16), it means that: -
(a)   You steal from people   (b)   You are a mischievous boy
(c)   You live in a warehouse   (d)   You don't have any parents

39)   Who was Sam Willis referring to in line 19 of the passage?
(a) His Lordship   (b) The King   (c) Mr. Walker   (d) Robert

40)   What does "flurry" mean (line 23)?
(a) Danger   (b) Commotion   (c) Accident   (d) Lack of

In the passage below various words are missing and a number has been put in their place. Read through the passage and work out what you think the missing word should be. Mark your answers on the separate answer sheet.

Matthew was usually a very happy boy, but (41) this occasion, something had upset him. His brother James tried to ask him what (42) matter was, but he would not say anything (43) him. His sister Julie also tried, but she had the (44) response. In the end his mother managed to coax out of (45) what the problem was. It was the (46) that he had been sleeping so deeply, that he missed (47) up in time to see one of his favourite TV programmes. It began at 8 o'clock in the morning, but it (48) until just before nine a.m. that Stuart (49) up, an (50) later than he expected to. "Never mind", said his mum, "I'm sure it will be repeated in the not too distant future".

In each line below choose one of the words in the brackets that makes the sentence read correctly. Mark your answers on the separate answer sheet.

51)   We did not understand the (compliant, complicated, composite) words.

52)   The police could only (specialise, specify, speculate) about the crash.

53)   The entertainer (contorted, continued, contradicted) his face.

54)   His doctor advised him to (seize, cease, sneeze) smoking.

55)   The man gave a very (articulate, artificial, arterial) speech.

56)   He enjoyed the concert (inversely, immensely, implicitly).

57)   The man started to (dislocate, dismay, dismantle) the chimney place.

58)   Your brother had a (unitary, unique, unison) collection of books.

END OF TEST PAPER TWO

PAPER 3

Read through the list of rules for walking in the mountains below and then answer the questions that follow. Mark your answers on the separate answer sheet.

<u>Safety Rules for Walkers Walking In The Mountains</u>

1) Make sure that you have suitable clothing and footwear. Your boots should have moulded grip-giving soles that can cope with rough ground. Thick socks should be worn over ordinary socks to avoid blisters. Wear several layers of clothing, which can be removed if it is warm. A windproof and waterproof jacket is essential.

5 2) Carry a rucksack which can contain food, drinks, first aid equipment (including medicines you might need) and a change of clothing. You should ideally have a vacuum flask containing hot tea or coffee as well as a full bottle of water. If you have a mobile phone use it only in emergencies. At all other times you should keep it switched off to preserve the life of the battery.

3) Bring along maps of the area you will be walking in. Different scale Ordnance Survey maps
10 such as 1:50,000 (2cm to 1km or 1.25 inches to the mile) and 1:25,000 (4cm to 1km or 2.5 inches to the mile) are recommended. Use the maps to plan your route and follow them during your walk.

4) Tell someone where you are going and what time you are expected back so that they can notify the Mountain Rescue Team if you are unduly late back.

5) Check the weather forecast before you start out and be prepared to turn back if the weather
15 changes for the worse.

6) Know your capabilities so that you don't over-exert yourself. If you find walking up the side of the mountain too strenuous, don't be afraid to change your route to an easier one. Don't take unnecessary risks such as jumping over a gully or crossing a stream.

7) Finally keep your wits about you at all times, looking out for potential dangers ahead. Keep to the footpaths at all times. Follow the Country Code.

1)   What does "essential" (line 4) mean?
        (a) Nice   (b) Necessary   (c) Optional   (d) Added

2)   What is a "rucksack" (line 5)?
        (a) A plastic bag   (b) A box   (c) A bag with straps   (d) A sack

3)   Why do you think carrying a mobile phone is good idea when walking in the mountains?
        (a) To speak to friends   (b) To send text messages
        (c) To let people contact you   (d) To call for help

4)   On a map with a scale of 1:50,000 what would 10 miles be?
        (a) 2 cms   (b) 4 cms   (c) 2.5 inches   (d) 12.5 inches

5)   When might the Mountain Rescue Team be notified according to the passage?
        (a)   If you are injured   (b)   If you haven't returned
        (c)   If you are lost   (d)   If you are stuck

6)   If the weather "changes for the worse" (line 15) what might it mean?
        (a)   It is sunny   (b)   It's windy
        (c)   It's raining lightly   (d)   It's raining heavily

7)   Another word for "capabilities" (line 16) would be: -
(a) Limits   (b) Strengths   (c) Routes   (d) Weaknesses

8)   What part of speech is "strenuous" (line 17)?
(a) Noun   (b) Verb   (c) Adjective   (d) Adverb

9)   What is a "gully" (line 18)?
(a) A path   (b) A gap   (c) A river   (d) A rock

10)   What does "potential" (line 19) mean?
(a) Possible   (b) Expected   (c) Hidden   (d) Dangerous

In the sentences below a noun has been written before a sentence. Change the noun into an adjective so that it fits in the missing space. Mark your answers on the separate answer sheet. *An example has been done for you.*

E.g.   Wonder   -   *He was reading a <u>wonderful</u> book*

11) Victory   -   It was a ________________ player who won the competition.
12) Drink   -   The intoxicated man became a ________________ lout.
13) Anger   -   The teacher had an ________________ word with the pupil.
14) Friend   -   We thought that you were a ________________ set of people.
15) Circle   -   I created a ________________ pattern in the book.
16) Giant   -   Their full back was a ________________ person.
17) Colour   -   We thought that it was a ________________ display.
18) Pot   -   My garden is full of ________________ plants.
19) Tattoo   -   I was shocked by the ________________ man.
20) Heart   -   The inebriated group sang a ________________ song.

In the lines below each word is part of a family. Work out what group it belongs to and mark your answers on the separate answer sheet. *An example has been done for you.*

E.g.   *Eagle, swan, thrush, pelican, albatross*   <u>*Birds*</u>

21) Square, circle, rectangle, rhombus, triangle
22) Minute, hour, second, week, month
23) Cotton, silk, denim, leather, wool
24) Iron, copper, tin, zinc, lead
25) India, Japan, Germany, Russia, Egypt
26) Orange, lemon, lime, raspberry, banana
27) Inch, centimetre, mile, foot, metre
28) Henry, Elizabeth, James, George, Victoria
29) Aunt, father, grandmother, cousin, nephew
30) Chicken, turkey, goose, duck

TURN OVER

Read through the passage below about a boy being kidnapped and then answer the questions that follow it. Mark your answers on the separate answer sheet.

As Stephen regained consciousness, he could not think straight. Where was he? Why was it dark? What was the strange noise that he could hear?
"He's waking up!", shouted a man's voice with a Cockney accent. Stephen started to lift his head up to see if he could see the person who had just spoken, but he was roughly pushed back into a
5 lying position. His heart began to beat faster.
"One move and you're dead meat, son!" said the same voice.
"Leave off him!" ordered another voice; this time it was female. "He won't harm no one. Not in the state he's in."
At that Stephen suddenly realised that the strange noise that he could hear in the background was
10 the noise of a helicopter approaching.
"Right son. In the next minute, yous and me 're gonna make a littul trip. All right? Off we go! But keep your head down."
The noise of the helicopter's whirring blades was deafening, adding to the splitting headache he already had. Also, its lights were incredibly bright, blindingly bright in fact, so that he was unable
15 to see the faces of his captors.
In no time at all he was in the helicopter, squashed between the woman and the man, sitting behind the pilot. Stephen felt his stomach rise up and then go down suddenly as the helicopter took off. Where was he going? What would happen to him?

31)   "Regained consciousness" (line 1) means that Stephen: -
      (a) Realised where he was   (b) Understood why he was being held
      (c) Woke up after being asleep   (d) None of these

32)   The man with a "Cockney accent" (line 3) meant that he came from: -
      (a) Liverpool   (b) London   (c) Birmingham   (d) Newcastle

33)   What part of speech is "roughly" (line 4)?
      (a) Noun   (b) Adjective   (c) Verb   (d) Adverb

34)   The way that the woman spoke to the man indicated that she: -
      (a) Did not like the boy   (b) Thought he could be dangerous
      (c) Was a clever boy   (d) Thought he wouldn't be a problem

35)   What means of transport was used to move Stephen?
      (a) Boat   (b) Helicopter   (c) Car   (d) Aeroplane

36)   "Whirring" (line 13) means:-
      (a) Buzzing   (b) Chiming   (c) Droning   (d) Humming

37)   Why do you think that Stephen had a "splitting headache"?
      (a) He'd fallen over   (b) He was very tired
      (c) He'd been hit on the head   (d) He had a migraine

38)   A "captor" (line 15) is someone who: -
      (a) Teaches you things   (b) Holds you prisoner
      (c) Gives you presents   (d) None of these

39)   At what time of the day do you think this episode took place?
        (a) Morning   (b) Lunchtime   (c) Afternoon   (d) During the night

40)   How many different people are mentioned in this extract?
        (a) Two   (b) Three   (c) Four   (d) Five

In the following sentences work out what the <u>plural</u> of the words underlined would be. Mark your answers on the separate answer sheet.

41)   I thought that the soldier was a brave <u>hero</u>.

42)   We laughed at the way the <u>shelf</u> fell down.

43)   The <u>sheep</u> grazed in the field.

44)   My friend gave me <u>half</u> of his orange.

45)   The <u>potato</u> originally came from America.

46)   In some countries they use an <u>ox</u> to pull a cart.

47)   The <u>deer</u> was lucky to miss being shot.

48)   He used the <u>brush</u> to sweep up the path.

49)   The tourist took pictures of the Indian <u>chief</u>.

50)   His <u>wife</u> was not very pleased with what he said.

Replace the words underlined in each sentence with a <u>similar meaning </u>word from the list below. Mark your answers on the separate answer sheet.

retire   rapid   just   obstinate   yield   weak   vacant   persuade   odour   rowdy

51)   The <u>puny</u> man could not stop the burglar from escaping.

52)   We had to <u>coax</u> the scared dog to come out of the pond.

53)   Sometimes donkeys can be <u>stubborn</u> and will not move.

54)   The injured footballer had to <u>withdraw</u> from the match.

55)   All judges are chosen for being <u>honest</u> and fair.

56)   There was an unpleasant <u>smell</u> coming from the bin.

57)   After the battle the defeated army had to <u>surrender</u>.

58)   The crafty man had a <u>quick</u> plan of escape.

59)   After the meeting there was a <u>noisy</u> crowd outside.

60)   The old house had remained <u>empty</u> for many years.

END OF TEST PAPER THREE

PAPER 4

Read through the passage below and then answer the questions that follow. Mark your answers on the separate answer sheet provided.

It was Katie who first noticed the smoke. She had always been a light sleeper and this particular night was no exception. She had heard the local church chime the strokes of midnight before dozing off into a fitful sleep. Soon after 1.00am she woke again. It was at this point that she remembered the warning bells going off in her head when she first smelt the smoke. It wasn't the
5   normal sort of smoke as with a bonfire, as it had a pungent smell which made her feel nauseous.
In an instant she knew it was smoke coming from something burning. She quickly got out of bed and put on the light just as the smoke alarm sounded in the hall downstairs. Immediately she could see wisps of smoke coming into the bedroom from underneath the bedroom door.
"Gemma!" she shouted at the top of her voice to her sleeping sister. Gemma stirred very slowly.
10   "Quick Gemma! We've got to get away. The house is on fire!
Gemma sat bolt upright in her bed. As the realisation of what was happening hit her, she started to panic and began screaming.
Luckily, the screams must have roused their parents as Katie heard the noise of approaching feet outside the door and then the door opening.
15   "Quick girls! There isn't a minute to lose!" shouted their father, bursting into their bedroom, followed by their mother.
"When I say 'run', I want you to run down the stairs and out of the front door holding your breath all the time".
By now the smoke was rushing in and both girls started to cough.
20   "Run!" shouted Dad and then all four of them took in a deep breath, before plunging through the thick, choking smoke, down the stairs and towards the front door.
It was very dark in spite of the light being on and everything seemed to be happening in slow motion. Eventually they came to the front door, which Dad somehow managed to open. One by one they plunged through into the cold and dark outside, pursued by the smoke. They were safe.

1)   How many strokes would the church bell chime for midnight?
     (a) Ten   (b) Eleven   (c) Twelve   (d) One

2)   What do you think "fitful" means (line 3)?
     (a) Strange   (b) Broken   (c) Peaceful   (d) Dreamy

3)   What does "pungent" (line 5) mean?
     (a) Sweet smelling   (b) Strange smelling
     (c) Strong smelling   (d) Sour smelling

4)   Why do you think the "wisps of smoke" were coming in the bedroom?
     (a) There was a breeze   (b) Pressure forced them
     (c) The door was open   (d) Smoke rises upwards

5)   What does "stirred" (line 9) mean?
     (a) Moved   (b) Walked   (c) Breathed   (d) Listened

6)   Why was Gemma screaming (line 12)?
     (a) She was having a nightmare   (b) She was scared
     (c) She saw a ghost   (d) She wanted help

7) What part of speech is "roused" (line 13)?
(a) Noun   (b) Adjective   (c) Verb   (d) Adverb

8) Why did Dad tell everyone to hold their breath (line 17)?
(a) To save their breath   (b) To stop inhaling the smoke
(c) To see who could last longest   (d) None of these

9) "Plunging" (line 20) means: -
(a) Push hard   (b) Drop   (c) Pierce   (d) Jump

10) "Pursued" (line 24) means: -
(a) Affected   (b) Choked   (c) Burnt   (d) Chased

In the sentences below, work out what the <u>opposite</u> of the underlined word would be, by adding one of these prefixes – dis il im in non un - to the front of the word. Mark your answers on the separate answer sheet *An example has been done for you.*

E.g.   *I didn't like what the <u>famous</u> actor had to say.*   *infamous*

11) We had an <u>advantage</u> over our opponents.

12) It was <u>proper</u> for my mother to tell him off.

13) The warrior had a <u>mortal</u> wound to his body.

14) It was <u>possible</u> to cross the river without danger.

15) They approached the footballer <u>legally.</u>

16) You were <u>polite</u> to the important visitor.

17) I <u>liked</u> the foreign visitor who visited our house.

18) The snake was a <u>poisonous</u> type.

19) We had to <u>twist</u> the lid very forcibly.

20) The loud music was <u>audible</u> from the street.

In the sentences below one of the words has been spelt incorrectly. Identify that word and then mark your choices on the separate answer sheet.

21) At the cafe I had a drink of orange juise.

22) In the end the army admited defeat.

23) My friend's neice came to stay last week.

24) The removal men dropped a valuble piece of furniture.

25) Your father rang to say he mist his train.

26) The committe managed to agree to the change.

27) Jack's horse galloped away in fright at the explosian.

28) The little boy was shocked at the sighte he saw.

29) I am quite good at mental arithmatic.

30) While they waited, one of them feinted.   **TURN OVER**

Read through the poem below and then answer the questions that follow it. Mark your answers on the separate answer sheet.

<u>The Wobbuliosaurus</u>

The Wobbuliosaurus is a most unusual sight.
You'd think it was shivering all over with contagious fright,
As it walks down the street, it sways from side to side,
Yet who would guess what this monster is like inside.
5 With long dangling brown hair and wide bulging green eyes,
A gignormous round stomach next to extra large thighs.
And in its enormous dense belly,
You will find a dense mass of jelly.

It lives on chocolate ice cream and chips with fried eggs,
10 Or anything full of fat like cheese and pig's legs.
It drinks beer by the gallon and wine by the litre.
And if it's still thirsty it has oil from a heater.
It does not have any friends or neighbours,
But every night it has to labour,
15 Until it is once again free
from the curse of the Evil Slee.

She it was who led Wobbuliosaurus to his sad fate.
By the light of the Full Moon was he cursed on that fateful date.
Poor creature is now being punished for being off its guard,
20 It must eat and eat until all that fat is made into lard.
Deep inside his brain this creature is never at peace
It wishes that one day its cravings to eat would cease.
But a knight will set him free from the curse,
And stop his condition from getting worse.

31) What does "contagious" (line 2) mean?
 (a) Unique (b) Catching (c) Strange (d) Special

32) What part of speech is the word "dangling" (line5)?
 (a) Noun (b) Verb (c) Adjective (d) Adverb

33) Which of the words below best describes what the Wobbuliosaurus is like?
 (a) Fat (b) Very fat (c) Average (d) Thin

34) What does "bulging" (line 5) mean?
 (a) Wide (b) Tall (c) Swelling (d) Tiny

35) Which word used in the poem is a slang word?
 (a) Ginormous (b) Bulging (c) Gallon (d) Lord

36)   Apart from beer and wine what else does the Wobbuliosaurus drink?
(a) Lard   (b) Cheese   (c) Oil   (d) Jelly

37)   What does the word "labour" (line 14) mean in the poem?
(a) Walk about   (b) Sleep   (c) Eat   (d) Work hard

38)   What is the curse that has been put on the Wobbuliosaurus?
(a) He must stay awake at night   (b) He must keep eating
(c) He must work all night   (d) He must try and stop eating

39)   How does the Wobbuliosaurus feel about his situation?
(a) Sad   (b) Happy   (c) He doesn't care   (d) Frustrated

40)   What does "cravings" (line 22) mean?
(a) Interests   (b) Hobbies   (c) Desires   (d) None of these

In the passage below certain words are missing. A number has been put in the place of the missing word. Read through the passage and then work out what you think the missing word should be. Mark your answers on the separate answer sheet.

It is (41) in the last hundred years or so that Sport has become popular the (42) over. Before then competitive sports did exist, but they were never organised in such a (43) as they are today. Take Football for instance. It is a sport that originated several hundred years ago in the Middle (44) where a pig's bladder would be inflated and players would have to (45) and get the ball from one end of their village to the (46). This game gradually developed into two distinct types - Rugby Football and Association (47). Today they are both played by millions of people the world over, with millions more (48) as spectators. Similarly, hockey, cricket, tennis and basketball have all developed (49) the years to the highly competitive sports that (50) are today. Athletics in all its various forms, both on the field and on the (51) has grown tremendously this century. No doubt, its growth has been (52) by the four yearly Olympic games, which were revived in 1896. Each (53) since, has been bigger than the last one, generating worldwide interest from (54) competitors and spectators alike. To win an Olympic Gold (55) is the ultimate achievement for any sportsman or sportswoman throughout the (56). Unfortunately, with so much at stake, there have been some who have resorted to (57) to achieve their aim. This has led to compulsory drugs testing after (58) event to check that a competitor is "clean" from any illegal (59) which may have been (60) to improve his or her performance.

END OF TEST PAPER FOUR

Notes For Parents

About the A Plus Series of Secondary School Entrance 11+ Practice Papers

The A Plus Series of Secondary School entrance practice papers have been designed to help children familiarise themselves with the wide variety of questions that are set in secondary school entrance examinations at age 11 or 12 for both state or private schools. Approximately twenty different types of English questions are covered in the two volumes so that your child will gain a wide experience of the types of questions that are usually set in these examinations. The questions are designed to be easier at first and then get harder as you go on, so that your child will not become disheartened. The practice papers are also designed to give your child the chance to work quickly and efficiently under timed conditions. The questions in Volume One are designed to be completed before Volume Two so that your child's understanding and confidence can be built up over the two volumes. With this set of English practice papers, the answers are set out in **multiple choice format.**

How to administer the practice papers

When your child sits these papers it is best to find a quiet place in the house where he or she will not be disturbed. It is also best to sit these papers at a time of day when your child is most mentally alert - usually in the morning after breakfast if at all possible.

This set of English practice papers contains separate answers sheets for your child to mark his/her answers on. Please cut/detach these from the back of this booklet. All your child has to do is to draw a short horizontal line <u>in pencil</u> across a small rectangular box (with a ruler if they wish). There is a choice of four or five possible answers for most questions, so your child needs to work out which answer s/he will choose from the question paper first of all. Most of the questions ask for just one answer, though there are some which require two answers. If s/he wants to change an answer, all s/he has to do is rub out the line and mark a new line in another box.

The timing of the tests is also equally important. Your child should be given 45 minutes to complete each English paper. It may be quite possible that for the first few tests your child will not have enough time to complete the whole test. This is understandable, as children need to learn to pace themselves, as well as become used to answering the different types of questions. If your child does not complete a paper, make a mark on the paper to show how far s/he has reached in 45 minutes, and then let him/her finish the rest of the questions in his/her own time. A good idea is to say when 20 minutes have passed and when there are 5 minutes to go. It is also important to emphasise that if your child finds that they cannot answer a question, they should put a mark in the margin of the question paper and not waste any more time attempting the question. Instead, if there is any time left, once they have finished the test, they should come back to that question. They are allowed to use any spare space on the question paper for working out their answers.

When marking the paper, there is always one mark for each correct answer, even if there are two parts to a particular question. The answers to the questions can be found on the next two pages.

Text © Mark Chatterton 1996/2006
English (Multiple Choice Format) Volume Two   ISBN 9781901146585
First published 1999   © MW Educational 1996/2006   This Edition 2011
Published by: MW Educational, Westcliff Drive, Leigh-on-Sea Essex SS9 2LB
Printed by: CPI Antony Rowe, 48-50 Birch Close, Eastbourne, East Sussex, BN23 6PE

ANSWERS: ENGLISH VOLUME 2 - PAPER ONE (MULTIPLE CHOICE)

1)	b	11)	I	21)	groans	31)	a
2)	d	12)	they	22)	whether	32)	c
3)	d	13)	we	23)	hoard	33)	d
4)	c	14)	you	24)	passed	34)	c
5)	a	15)	our	25)	pair	35)	c
6)	b	16)	himself	26)	site	36)	c
7)	d	17)	she	27)	thrown	37)	b
8)	a	18)	who	28)	tales	38)	d
9)	b	19)	they're	29)	d	39)	b
10)	b	20)	heard	30)	b		

40) My father told me to come and watch the <u>game</u>

41) For breakfast I had bacon and egg with <u>toast</u>

42) We go to the park in <u>Summer</u>

43) I didn't like the way I was spoken <u>to</u>

44) My best friend remembered my <u>birthday</u>

45) We enjoyed listening to the music which they <u>played</u>

46) The frightened animal was rescued by the kind <u>girl</u>

47) Every year my brother and I go strawberry <u>picking</u>

ANSWERS: ENGLISH VOLUME 2 - PAPER TWO (MULTIPLE CHOICE)

1)	c	16)	'	31)	c	46)	fact
2)	c	17)	,	32)	b	47)	getting
3)	d	18)	?	33)	d	48)	wasn't
4)	d	19)	.	34)	a	49)	woke
5)	b	20)	hard	35)	c	50)	hour
6)	a	21)	slowly	36)	b	51)	complicated
7)	b	22)	hardly	37)	c	52)	speculate
8)	d	23)	badly	38)	b	53)	contorted
9)	b	24)	bravely	39)	b	54)	cease
10)	'	25)	lovingly	40)	b	55)	articulate
11)	?	26)	mockingly	41)	on	56)	immensely
12)	,	27)	later	42)	the	57)	dismantle
13)	.	28)	quite	43)	to	58)	unique
14)	""	29)	once	44)	same		
15)	""	30)	b	45)	him		

<u>**ANSWERS: ENGLISH VOLUME 2 - PAPER THREE (MULTIPLE CHOICE)**</u>

1)	b	16)	gigantic	31)	c	46)	oxen
2)	c	17)	colourful	32)	b	47)	deer
3)	d	18)	potted	33)	d	48)	brushes
4)	d	19)	tattooed	34)	d	49)	chiefs
5)	b	20)	hearty	35)	b	50)	wives
6)	d	21)	shapes	36)	a	51)	weak
7)	a	22)	time	37)	c	52)	persuade
8)	c	23)	materials	38)	b	53)	obstinate
9)	b	24)	metals	39)	d	54)	retire
10)	a	25)	countries	40)	c	55)	just
11)	victorious	26)	fruits	41)	heroes	56)	odour
12)	drunken	27)	units (of length)	42)	shelves	57)	yield
13)	angry	28)	monarchs	43)	sheep	58)	rapid
14)	friendly	29)	relatives	44)	halves	59)	rowdy
15)	circular	30)	poultry	45)	potatoes	60)	vacant

<u>**ANSWERS: ENGLISH VOLUME 2 - PAPER FOUR (MULTIPLE CHOICE)**</u>

1)	c	16)	im	31)	b	46)	other
2)	b	17)	dis	32)	c	47)	football
3)	d	18)	non	33)	b	48)	watching
4)	b	19)	un	34)	c	49)	over
5)	a	20)	in	35)	a	50)	they
6)	b	21)	juise	36)	c	51)	track
7)	c	22)	admited	37)	d	52)	influenced
8)	b	23)	neice	38)	b	53)	games
9)	a	24)	valuble	39)	d	54)	both
10)	d	25)	mist	40)	c	55)	medal
11)	dis	26)	committe	41)	only	56)	world
12)	im	27)	explosian	42)	world	57)	cheating
13)	im	28)	sighte	43)	way	58)	very
14)	im	29)	arithmatic	44)	Ages	59)	drugs
15)	il	30)	feinted	45)	try	60)	taken

PUPIL ANSWER SHEET FOR PAPER 1

PLEASE MARK YOUR ANSWERS IN PENCIL ONLY. DRAW A STRAIGHT LINE ACROSS THE BOX NEXT TO THE ANSWER THAT YOU CHOOSE. IF YOU WISH TO CHANGE AN ANSWER RUB IT OUT AND PUT A FRESH LINE IN A DIFFERENT SPACE. THERE IS AN EXAMPLE TO HELP YOU

Eg) A B C D

1) A B C D

2) A B C D

3) A B C D

4) A B C D

5) A B C D

6) A B C D

7) A B C D

8) A B C D

9) A B C D

10) A B C D

11) I / like / the / way / man

12) when / the / saw / they / away

13) after / supper / we / to / the

14) the / rules / state / you / not

15) our / friends / very / well / the

16) the / was / cross / himself / for

17) what / the / she / move / way

18) who / saw / the / intruder / officer

19) they're / their

20) herd / heard

21) growns / groans

22) whether / weather

23) hoard / horde

24) past / passed

25) pair / pear

26) sight / site

27) thrown / throne

28) tails / tales

29) A B C D

30) A B C D

31) A B C D

32) A B C D

33) A B C D

34) A B C D

35) A B C D

36) A B C D

37) A B C D

38) A B C D

39) A B C D

40) come / told / watch / father / game

41) toast / with / egg / bacon / breakfast

42) the / park / summer / go / to

43) way / was / spoken / like / to

44) friend / my / birthday / remembered / best

45) they / played / listening / music / enjoyed

46) kind / frightened / girl / rescued / animal

47) strawberry / picking / and / brother / year

END OF THE PUPIL ANSWER SHEET FOR PAPER ONE

PUPIL ANSWER SHEET FOR PAPER 2

PLEASE MARK YOUR ANSWERS IN PENCIL ONLY. DRAW A STRAIGHT LINE ACROSS THE BOX NEXT TO THE ANSWER THAT YOU CHOOSE. IF YOU WISH TO CHANGE AN ANSWER RUB IT OUT AND PUT A FRESH LINE IN A DIFFERENT SPACE. THERE IS AN EXAMPLE TO HELP YOU

1) A B C D

2) A B C D

3) A B C D

4) A B C D

5) A B C D

6) A B C D

7) A B C D

8) A B C D

9) A B C D

10) , . ; ? " "

11) , . ; ? " "

12) , . ; ? " "

13) , . ; ? " "

14) , . ; ? " "

15) , . ; ? " "

16) , . ; ? " "

17) , . ; ? " "

18) , . ; ? " "

19) , . ; ? " "

Eg
fat
running
slowly ■
exhausted

20) couldn't / find / despite / hard

21) Don't / walk / slowly / shouted

22) hardly / clever / enough / solve

23) best / friend / failed / badly

24) soldiers / fought / bravely / enemy

25) neighbour / worked / lovingly / garden

26) couldn't / understand / laughed / mockingly

27) bus / arrived / later / expected

28) quite / nice / playing / snow

29) They / once / visited / barrier

30) A B C D

31) A B C D

32) A B C D

33) A B C D

34) A B C D

35) A B C D

36) A B C D

37) A B C D

38) A B C D

39) A B C D

40) A B C D

41) was / on / the

42) was / it / the

43) by / at / to

44) right / same / wrong

45) him / her / it

46) was / problem / fact

47) moving / getting / sleeping

48) was / wasn't / happened

49) woke / rose / moved

50) minute / hour / day

51) compliant / complicated / composite

52) specialise / specify / speculate

53) contorted / continued / contradicted

54) seize / cease / sneeze

55) articulate / artificial / arterial

56) inversely / immensely / implicitly

57) dislocate / dismay / dismantle

58) unitary / unique / unison

END OF THE PUPIL ANSWER SHEET FOR PAPER TWO

PUPIL ANSWER SHEET FOR PAPER 3

PLEASE MARK YOUR ANSWERS IN PENCIL ONLY. DRAW A STRAIGHT LINE ACROSS THE BOX NEXT TO THE ANSWER THAT YOU CHOOSE. IF YOU WISH TO CHANGE AN ANSWER RUB IT OUT AND PUT A FRESH LINE IN A DIFFERENT SPACE. THERE ARE EXAMPLES TO HELP YOU.

1) A B C D

2) A B C D

3) A B C D

4) A B C D

5) A B C D

6) A B C D

7) A B C D

8) A B C D

9) A B C D

10) A B C D

Eg wondering / **wonderful** / wonderous / wonderly

11) victory / victorary / victionary / victorious

12) drunk / drunken / **drank** / drinking

13) angrous / angree / **anger** / angry

14) friends / friendly / friendish / friendy

15) circlous / circling / circular / circly

16) giantic / gigantic / giantly / giantous

17) colourful / colouring / colourly / colourous

18) potty / poted / potted / poting

19) tatoed / tatooed / tattoed / tattooed

20) hearted / hearty / heartful / heartly

Eg animals / **birds** / hunters

21) angles / objects / shapes

22) sizes / time / order

23) clothes / materials / weaving

24) metals / materials / mixtures

25) capitals / counties / countries

26) colours / fruits / tastes

27) metric / imperial / units

28) kings / queens / monarchs

29) friends / relatives / parents

30) poultry / meals / pets

31) A B C D

32) A B C D

33) A B C D

34) A B C D

35) A B C D

36) A B C D

37) A B C D

38) A B C D

39) A B C D

40) A B C D

41) heros / heroes / heroine

42) shelfs / shelfes / shelves

43) sheep / sheeps / sheepes

44) halfs / halfes / halves

45) potatos / potatoes / potato

46) oxes / oxen / ox

47) deer / deers / deeres

48) brushs / brushis / brushes

49) chiefs / chicfcs / chieves

50) wifes / wivs / wives

51) rowdy / obstinate / weak

52) yield / persuade / retire

53) rowdy / obstinate / weak

54) yield / persuade / retire

55) vacant / just / rowdy

56) odour / rapid / retire

57) yield / persuade / retire

58) odour / rapid / retire

59) rowdy / obstinate / weak

60) vacant / just / rowdy

END OF THE PUPIL ANSWER SHEET FOR PAPER THREE

PUPIL ANSWER SHEET FOR PAPER 4

PLEASE MARK YOUR ANSWERS IN PENCIL ONLY. DRAW A STRAIGHT LINE ACROSS THE BOX NEXT TO THE ANSWER THAT YOU CHOOSE. IF YOU WISH TO CHANGE AN ANSWER RUB IT OUT AND PUT A FRESH LINE IN A DIFFERENT SPACE. THERE IS AN EXAMPLE TO HELP YOU.

1) A B C D   2) A B C D   3) A B C D   4) A B C D   5) A B C D   6) A B C D   7) A B C D

8) A B C D   9) A B C D   10) A B C D

Eg) dis / in (■) / il / non / im / un

11) dis / in / il / non / im / un

12) dis / in / il / non / im / un

13) dis / in / il / non / im / un

14) dis / in / il / non / im / un

15) dis / in / il / non / im / un

16) dis / in / il / non / im / un

17) dis / in / il / non / im / un

18) dis / in / il / non / im / un

19) dis / in / il / non / im / un

20) dis / in / il / non / im / un

21) cafe / drink / orange / juise

22) end / army / admited / defeat

23) friend's / neice / came / week

24) removal / valuble / piece / furniture

25) father / rang / mist / furniture

26) committe / managed / agree / change

27) horse / galloped / fright / explosian

28) little / shocked / sighte / saw

29) quite / good / mental / arithmatic

30) while / waited / them / feinted

31) A B C D   32) A B C D   33) A B C D   34) A B C D   35) A B C D   36) A B C D   37) A B C D

38) A B C D   39) A B C D   40) A B C D

41) since / only / in

42) earth / all / world

43) order / process / way

44) times / ages / period

45) try / aim / have

46) next / near / other

47) rugby / football / cricket

48) standing / watching / looking

49) over / in / above

50) you / we / they

51) river / track / field

52) used / seen / influenced

53) games / sport / olympic

54) both / every / all

55) prize / win / medal

56) area / world / event

57) winning / trying / cheating

58) every / all / most

59) pills / drugs / drinks

60) bought / given / taken

END OF THE PUPIL ANSWER SHEET FOR PAPER FOUR